A FIREFLY BOOK

Published by Firefly Books Ltd. 2018

Original Spanish-edition copyright © 2018, Combel Editorial, S. A.

This English-edition copyright © 2018 Firefly Books
Text copyright © 2018 Jaume Copons
Illustrations copyright © 2018 Mercè Galí

First printing

Publisher Cataloging-in-Publication Data (U.S.)

Library of Congress Control Number: 2018932972

Library and Archives Canada Cataloguing in Publication

Copons, Jaume, 1966-, author
    Everything I know about poop / Jaume Copons, Mercè Galí.
ISBN 978-0-228-10083-6 (softcover)
    1. Feces--Juvenile literature. I. Galí, Mercè, illustrator II. Title.
QP159.C67 2018   j612.3'6   C2018-900851-2

Published in the United States by
Firefly Books (U.S.) Inc.
P.O. Box 1338, Ellicott Station
Buffalo, New York 14205

Published in Canada by
Firefly Books Ltd.
50 Staples Avenue, Unit 1
Richmond Hill, Ontario L4B 0A7

Translator: Lionel Koffler

Printed in China

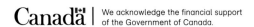 We acknowledge the financial support of the Government of Canada.

First published in Catalan and Spanish by Combel Editorial, SA
Casp, 79 – 08013 Barcelona
Original title: Tot el que sé de la caca

Everything I Know About POOP

JAUME COPONS

MERCÈ GALÍ

FIREFLY BOOKS

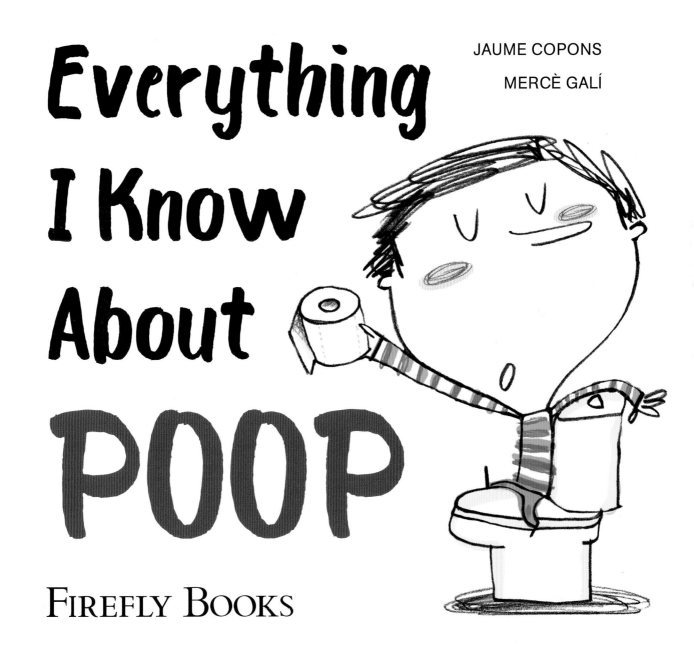

Everyone knows how
to make a nice poop!

And people who do not
know, learn sooner or later.

If you poop raise your hand!

me!

Our little brother poops...

ME!

Mom and Dad also poop.

ME!

Even grandma and grandpa still poop!

A hippo poops.

With its tail spinning like a helicopter,
it flings poop through the air.

Yuck!
What a mess it makes!

Birds know how to poop.

Onto people, sometimes.
(But not on me!)

Grandma has a cute puppy that
poops anywhere on the street.

You have to pick it up,
and throw it away.

(The poop,
not the dog.)

While our very proud cat
prefers to poop in his litter box.

Cows make huge poops,
like a pizza!

And goats make little balls, like olives.

Insects make tiny poops
that you hardly ever see.

While some beetles roll poop into big balls.

You should see elephant poops! They're huge!

And so is what whales do in the ocean.

What about me?
What about you?
How do we poop?

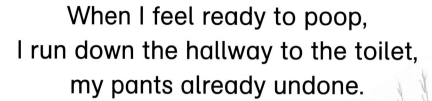

When I feel ready to poop,
I run down the hallway to the toilet,
my pants already undone.

I sit on the toilet, calm and patient.

Oh, if there's no toilet paper,
I ask my sister for a roll.

Sometimes a few little farts escape,

but nothing else happens.

Once in a while, I have a hard time,
and my face gets red from the effort.

In these cases, a little cheering is always welcome.

And, suddenly...

PLOP!

What a relief!

Yay!
A very nice poop!

My whole family is very happy for me... and my poop!

I say goodbye to my poop.
I use my fingertips to flush,
and then wash and dry my hands.

There, now you know as
much as I do about poop!

For little Júlia Sanarau, who fills
our days with smiles... and poop!
M. G.